ONE LONG LINE

ONE LONG LINE

Marching Caterpillars and the Scientists Who Followed Them

Loree Griffin Burns

illustrated by Jamie Green

≡mit **Kids** Press

To Stan Selkow, who introduced me to Henri, and
to Deb Selkow, who introduced me to Stan
LGB

To Emily and M, the two people who I can count on to
call me outside if there's a worm on the pavement
JG

Text copyright © 2024 by Loree Griffin Burns
Illustrations copyright © 2024 by Jamie Green

This book would not exist without the generosity of Dr. Terrence Fitzgerald,
distinguished professor at the State University of New York at Cortland; thank you, Terry.
The author would like to thank Lea Morgan, manager of exhibitions at the
New England Botanic Garden at Tower Hill, and Dr. Elizabeth Barnes,
exotic forest pest educator at Purdue University, for sharing their expertise.

The MIT Press, the ☰mit Kids Press colophon, and MIT Kids Press are
trademarks of The MIT Press, a department of the Massachusetts Institute of Technology,
and used under license from The MIT Press. The colophon and MIT Kids Press are
registered in the US Patent and Trademark Office.

First edition 2024

Library of Congress Catalog Card Number 2023944788
ISBN 978-1-5362-2868-7

24 25 26 27 28 29 APS 10 9 8 7 6 5 4 3 2 1

Printed in Humen, Dongguan, China

This book was typeset in Museo Slab.
The illustrations were created digitally.

MIT Kids Press
an imprint of Candlewick Press
99 Dover Street
Somerville, Massachusetts 02144

mitkidspress.com
candlewick.com

Contents

INTRODUCTION   1

CHAPTER ONE: The Caterpillar   7

CHAPTER TWO: The Procession   11

CHAPTER THREE: The Leader   15

CHAPTER FOUR: The Circle   19

CHAPTER FIVE: Tricked?   23

CHAPTER SIX: A Quarter Century Later   27

CHAPTER SEVEN: Silk-less Caterpillars   31

CHAPTER EIGHT: Trail   35

CHAPTER NINE: No Trail   40

CHAPTER TEN: A Sacrifice   43

CHAPTER ELEVEN: Trapped!   47

CONCLUSION   50

GLOSSARY   52

MORE ABOUT JEAN-HENRI FABRE AND TERRENCE FITZGERALD   54

FURTHER READING   54

SOURCE NOTES   55

BIBLIOGRAPHY   56

Introduction

This is a story about unusual caterpillars, curious people, and fascinating conversations.

The caterpillars are called pine processionaries. *Pine* because they live in pine trees, and *processionary* because wherever they go, they go in long single-file lines. Processions.

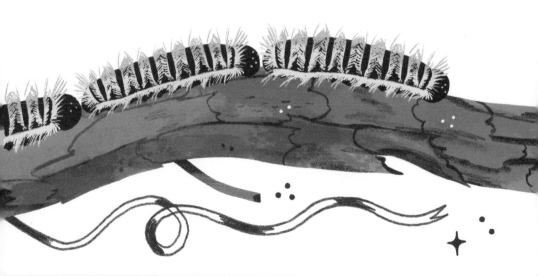

The people are Jean-Henri Fabre, a Frenchman who died in 1915,

and Terrence Fitzgerald, an American who was born twenty-six years later, in 1941.

The fascinating conversations? Wordless.

Because caterpillars can't talk, of course. And neither can men who worked and wondered in different centuries! Still, Henri and Terrence, in their own days and in their own ways, managed to chat with pine processionary caterpillars.

Why do you move that way? they asked.

And how?

They posed these questions in the language of science, through carefully designed experiments.

The caterpillars? They answered.

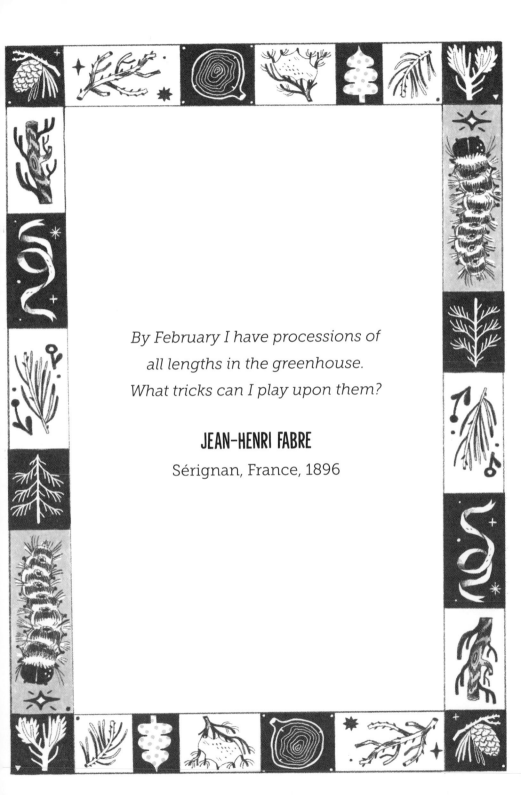

By February I have processions of
all lengths in the greenhouse.
What tricks can I play upon them?

JEAN-HENRI FABRE

Sérignan, France, 1896

One

THE CATERPILLAR

Jean-Henri Fabre was already fifty-six years old when his dream of a backyard laboratory came true. He'd been studying the plants and insects of southern France for his whole life, even though his teaching schedule left him very little time for the work. But suddenly, in the middle of his life, he caught a break: the science textbooks he'd begun writing became a success. The money he made was

enough to buy a house with a yard. And Henri knew just what he wanted to do with that yard: let it go wild.

Henri didn't plant a vegetable garden, or put in tidy rows of flowers, or even trim his bushes. He didn't fertilize the soil or cut the grass. He did nothing at all that would make his yard pleasant for people. Instead, he let thistles and couch grasses take over the red, pebbly earth. He encouraged a thicket of brambles. And he welcomed the wasps and beetles and flies and ants and butterflies and moths that came to live.

The pine processionary caterpillars that moved into Henri's yard didn't know they would be part of his science experiments. They knew only what all caterpil-lars know: how to hatch from an egg, how to eat leaves, and how to molt, pupate, and even- tually emerge as adult moths. Caterpillars live out this life cycle instinctually. They don't have to think about it—they just do it. Once some of them began doing it in Henri's yard, he launched a study of the pine processionary life.

In the fall, Henri watched female pine processionary moths lay hundreds of eggs on the needles of his pine trees.

When those eggs hatched, Henri watched the cater-pillars that emerged munch on pine needles. He saw them weave nests at the tops of the trees. He noticed that the caterpillars ate all the needles near their nest first and, so, were eventually forced to travel farther and farther to find pine needles for dinner. Henri took notes as they lined up to march.

"Where the first goes all the others go . . ." Henri wrote of these processions. "They proceed in a single file, in a continuous row, each touching with its head the rear of the one in front of it."

TO EACH THEIR OWN

Henri didn't drug the bugs in his yard, pin them to cork tiles, or dissect their parts, as scientists in his day often did. He preferred to watch them alive and well and busy with the small industries of their insect lives. Whenever he wondered about some habit he saw, he designed experiments to help him understand it. These experiments were almost always carried out right there in his yard, on living insects in their natural habitats.

Two

THE PROCESSION

When Henri's neighbors noticed pine processionary caterpillar nests in the tops of their pine trees,
they cut the nests out and burned them. They knew that
too many hungry caterpillars meant too much devouring of pine needles. They knew that too much devouring
of pine needles could kill a tree.

Henri sometimes cut the nests from his trees, too.
But he took the cut branches (and the caterpillar nests in
them) to his backyard greenhouse, where he set them in
large pots. Now he could study pine processionary caterpillars and their marching habits closely. One of the
first things he noticed was that the caterpillars spread
silk wherever they marched.

The caterpillar at the head of the procession laid a silken thread underfoot. The next caterpillar in the parade added its own thread to the one laid down by the first, doubling its thickness. The third caterpillar tripled it. And so on and so on.

"When the procession has marched by," Henri wrote, "there remains, as a record of its passing, a narrow white ribbon."

Night after night, Henri went to the greenhouse to watch the caterpillars sally forth from their nests, laying a road of silk as they did. When the procession reached a spray of needles on which to feed, the individual caterpillars spread out among the needles to graze. When they'd had their fill, the caterpillars found the silk strand they'd laid earlier and followed it single file, straight back to the nest.

By following this silk ribbon, Henri guessed, the processionaries made their way home without ever losing their way.

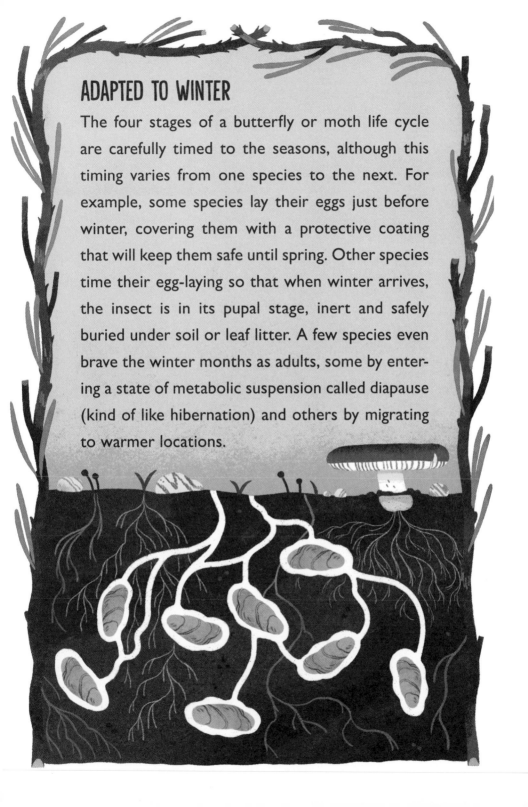

ADAPTED TO WINTER

The four stages of a butterfly or moth life cycle are carefully timed to the seasons, although this timing varies from one species to the next. For example, some species lay their eggs just before winter, covering them with a protective coating that will keep them safe until spring. Other species time their egg-laying so that when winter arrives, the insect is in its pupal stage, inert and safely buried under soil or leaf litter. A few species even brave the winter months as adults, some by entering a state of metabolic suspension called diapause (kind of like hibernation) and others by migrating to warmer locations.

Spending the bitter-cold winter of life as a fragile, soft-bodied, perpetually famished caterpillar, however, is something very few butterflies or moths can pull off. The temperature at which an organism is no longer able to move or function due to cold is known as its chill coma. And because pine processionaries have one of the lowest chill comas ever documented for an insect, they are one of the few species that overwinter as caterpillars.

Three

THE LEADER

There were other caterpillar habits that tickled Henri's curiosity. The strange thrashing habit of line leaders, for example. While most of the caterpillars marched serenely in line, the movement of the front-most caterpillar was more complicated. This caterpillar lifted the front of its body off the ground, laid it down to one side of its walking path, lifted it again, and laid it down on the other side of its walking path. By this lifting and swinging, the leader seemed to choose a route for the procession.

Was the caterpillar at the front the only one that could move this way? Was the leader specially trained for the job of choosing a path? Was the leader the oldest caterpillar in the family? The fittest? Special in some other way? Can any caterpillar be a line leader? Do they take turns?

Henri wondered how best to ask the caterpillars these questions.

As he watched his processions by the light of a lantern in his greenhouse, shivering in the winter chill, he thought hard about which was the most important of these questions—and what experiment would allow him to ask it. Eventually, he settled on this one:

CAN THE SECOND CATERPILLAR BE A LINE LEADER, TOO?

Henri waited for a procession to leave the nest, and then he lifted the line leader up and separated it from the rest of the line. He watched to see what the second caterpillar would do.

The second caterpillar immediately took up the movements of a leader: it lifted its body and swung it from side to side, searching for a good path forward. It was as if the second caterpillar had said, *Yes, I can be a line leader, too.*

Henri repeated this experiment many times on many procfessions of caterpillars. The results were always the same: the second caterpillar in line is perfectly capable of leading a procession.

Right away, Henri wondered about the other caterpillars in a line. The next question came to him quickly.

HENRI'S HELPERS

Henri and his wife, Marie, had six children. Their oldest, a son, died as an infant. Antonia, Claire, Aglaé, Emile, and Jules grew up studying their insect neighbors with Henri. Years later, when Marie died and the older children had left home, Henri married again. His second wife and their three children—Paul, Marie-Pauline, and Anna—became Henri's companions and collaborators. Henri's books are filled with stories of all his kids and their many, many adventures with insects.

Four

THE CIRCLE

CAN CATERPILLARS IN THE MIDDLE OF A PROCESSION BE LEADERS, TOO?

Once again, Henri waited in his greenhouse for a long procession. This time he gently lifted a caterpillar from the middle of the passing parade. Using a brush made of horsehair, he wiped away the silken strand beneath the spot where the middle caterpillar had been. Then he watched to see what the two processions in front of him would do.

The caterpillar at the front of the line continued to lead its half of the procession.

The caterpillar now at the head of the second line, so recently a follower, immediately began to move like a leader. It lifted its body and swung it first to one side and then to the other.

As before, Henri repeated this experiment many times, with processions of all lengths, testing caterpillars all along the line. Their answer was unanimous: any caterpillar can lead, so long as it's at the front of a procession.

This answer, too, led Henri to more questions. For example, how strong were these caterpillar instincts to lead and to follow? Henri had seen that caterpillars in the front of a line always led. Now he wanted to know:

WILL CATERPILLARS IN THE BACK ALWAYS FOLLOW?

In other words, were there any conditions under which the caterpillars might abandon this instinct? What would the caterpillars do, for example, if they had a lousy leader—or no line leader at all? What if a leader were to march around to the end of its own procession, join it, and become a follower? Could Henri trick a procession into forming such a circle? What would happen if he did?

Henri attempted to make a circle of caterpillars many, many times. Forceps in hand, he followed procession after procession around his greenhouse, trying to force the leader to meet up with the back of its own line. But each time, no matter how steady Henri's hand, no matter how long the line of caterpillars, the procession fell apart.

But then, one sunny and splendid winter's day in January of 1896, Henri discovered a procession of some length marching up the side of a pot in his greenhouse. At the top of the climb, the troop began to march in a circle around the pot's rim. Henri realized this was just the opportunity he needed.

As the leader of the pot-climbers made its way to the end of the circle, to the spot on the rim where its own followers were still climbing up the side of the pot, Henri bent close with his brush. Just as the leader reached the climbers, Henri brushed the climbers and the silk road they were climbing clean away.

And, so, the leader met up with the end of its own line.

Voilà! A circle of marching caterpillars! With no leader!

What would the caterpillars do now?

Five

TRICKED?

"he procession will go on turning for some time, for an hour, two hours perhaps; then the caterpillars will perceive their mistake. They will abandon the deceptive road and make their descent somewhere or other."

This was Henri's prediction.

It's not what happened.

Incredibly, the leaderless march of the pine processionary caterpillars lasted for more than a week! During this time, the caterpillars did not eat. They rested fitfully, when cold or fatigue or hunger temporarily overcame their instinct to march. But always the circle reformed, and the march resumed.

"All follow mechanically, as faithful to their circle as are the hands of a watch," Henri wrote.

Finally, on the eighth day, a tired and famished caterpillar slip-stepped off the silk-lined rim of the pot. A few of those behind it followed, weakly. Eventually the entire troop took up the trail this poor creature had blazed, and the weary caterpillars found their way back to their nest. Henri calculated that they had circled the rim of the pot 365 times, a march of more than one quarter mile.

Henri ended his work on the pine processionary marching habits here. Perhaps he was distracted by the many other questions he had for these creatures; he went on to study their eggs, their communal nests, the adult moths, and more. Maybe he got tied up with his experiments on spiders, beetles, flies, bees, wasps, grass-hoppers, and other backyard insects.

Or perhaps he felt he'd figured it all out.

He'd shown that pine processionary caterpillars were born with a simple two-part marching instinct. If a caterpillar found itself at the front of the line, it led. If a caterpillar found itself behind another caterpillar, it followed. When he died in 1915, nearly two decades after his processionary circle experiment, Henri believed that their marching habit was built entirely on silk.

But it wasn't.

SOUVENIRS ENTOMOLOGIQUES

Henri was an excellent naturalist; Charles Darwin once called him an "inimitable observer." He was also a gifted storyteller, one the French novelist Victor Hugo called "the insect's Homer." Henri published his lifetime of insect and arachnid studies in a ten-book collection that includes volumes on grasshoppers, bees, caterpillars, scorpions, beetles, spiders, flies, and wasps. These volumes have been translated into dozens of languages, including English, and they are seriously good reads.

Six

A QUARTER CENTURY LATER

Terrence Fitzgerald was born in America twenty-six years after Henri died in France. He grew up in Buffalo, New York, where his favorite thing to do was find wildlife. He explored undeveloped fields around the city whenever he could, learning about the birds, insects, and other creatures that called Buffalo home, too. When the time came for Terrence to go to college, he decided to make a

career of studying insects. His specialty became tent caterpillars.

Like processionaries, tent caterpillars live in communal tree nests built with their own silk. They live and feed together, sometimes travel together, and often lay silk together. But tent caterpillars are much less orderly in their togetherness. They don't march together in long lines. They don't form processions.

tent caterpillar

pine processionary

In his work with tent caterpillars, Terrence had learned that other methods of communication were more important than silk—like the spreading of chemicals. Plants and animals produce their own chemicals, called pheromones, and use them to send messages to one another. African acacia trees being munched on by giraffes, for example, release chemicals that nearby acacia trees detect and respond to by making their own leaves less tasty to giraffes. Some female moths release mating pheromones that can be detected by male moths several miles away, causing the males to immediately fly in the females' direction.

Terrence had shown in laboratory experiments that tent caterpillars mark their paths to and from plentiful food sources with pheromones. They do this by dragging their abdomens, where the pheromones are produced, over the ground they're walking on. Sibling caterpillars can later follow these chemical trails to find the food.

So Terrence wondered what role pheromones might have played in Henri's processionary experiments. He couldn't ask Henri about it, of course, because he had been dead for a long time. But . . . could he ask Henri's caterpillars? Or to be more accurate, could he ask their descendants? Pine processionary caterpillars don't live in America, so if Terrence did want to ask them about pheromones and their processionary habits, he'd have to go to Europe.

And, so, he did.

CHECK YOUR TREETOPS!

There are more than three hundred species of social caterpillars—ones that live in large sibling groups—around the world. Terrence, who turned eighty years old in 2021, is still curious about all of them. In fact, he keeps a public website with lots of information on the species that march in strict single files, like the pine processionaries, and the species that are more loosey-goosey in their travel habits, like his beloved tent caterpillars. That website includes this exciting tidbit, aimed especially at the scientifically minded visitor: "To date, the social behavior of only a dozen or so of these species has been investigated in any detail."

Seven

SILK-LESS CATERPILLARS

Terrence arrived in Catalonia, Spain, in February, when local pine processionary caterpillars were nearly full-grown and actively preparing for the biggest change in any caterpillar's life: pupation. During the pupal stage of life, a caterpillar's fat, many-legged, silk-dribbling body changes into the thinner, hairier, scaly-winged body of an adult moth.

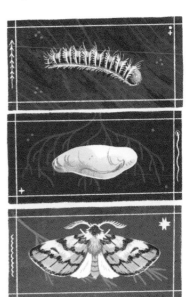

Terrence spent ten days in Catalonia watching pine

processionary caterpillars eat their final caterpillar meals. He followed remarkable single-file processions—some more than 20 feet (6 meters) long and containing hundreds of individual caterpillars—as they marched out of pine trees and snaked across the dry ground, searching for a safe place to pupate. When the caterpillars had found those safe places, Terrence watched them dig themselves down into the dirt. Safely buried, near to one another as always, individual pine processionary caterpillars would then spin silk cocoons. They were no longer caterpillars but not quite moths yet. They were something in between: pine processionary pupae. They would be pupae for the next five months, so Terrence went back to America for the spring and the summer.

In August, he returned to Spain. He arrived just as adult pine processionary moths began digging themselves out of the ground.

He watched as males and females found one another and mated.

He watched as pregnant females laid hundreds of eggs on the needles of nearby pine trees.

And soon after that, he clipped dozens and dozens of egg-coated pine needles, packed them carefully, and flew them back to his laboratory in America. In his luggage! (Don't worry. He had all the necessary permits.)

As he traveled back home and waited for the eggs to hatch, Terrence planned experiments that would allow the caterpillars to tell him if their processionary habits were dependent on silk, on pheromones, or on both. He decided it would be convenient to work with pine processionary caterpillars that didn't make any silk. And since silk-less pine processionary caterpillars didn't exist, he decided this, too: he would make them.

BEWARE THE HAIRS

Hairy caterpillars are rather common, and often their hairs can cause allergic reactions in people. Handle them with care, especially if the hairy caterpillar in question is a pine processionary. Henri learned early on that the hairs could cause an itchy, irritated rash on human skin. And because Henri was Henri, he studied this aspect of pine processionary hairs extensively, handling uncountable caterpillars and later writing that their hairy exoskeletons were "a poisoned fabric [that] sets fire to the fingers that handle it." We now know that the hairs are stiff, sharp-pointed bristles that pierce skin and release a toxin. Terrence has written that "there were few days during my studies when I didn't have to deal with an itching dermatitis."

Eight
TRAIL

The caterpillar organ for producing silk, the spinneret, is located underneath the animal's head. When the eggs Terrence brought back from Spain hatched, he fed the tiny caterpillars pine needles and watched them grow. When they were big enough to handle, he collected two groups of thirty caterpillars each.

He put a drop of glue on the tip of the spinneret of each caterpillar in one group.

He left the spinnerets of the caterpillars in the other group alone.

Then he put each group on a separate sheet of white paper and watched to see what they would do.

Both groups of caterpillars, the ones with plugged spinnerets and the ones without, formed lines and marched over the page. Both were capable of processioning.

So Terrence followed each group of processioning caterpillars with a pencil in his hand, placing dots behind the last caterpillar in line as it followed the troop across the page. When the caterpillars had marched off, Terrence examined each sheet of paper under a microscope, looking for silk.

The pine processionaries with untouched spinnerets had laid a trail of silk that exactly coincided with the dotted pencil line.

The pine processionaries with plugged spinnerets had laid no silk at all.

Terrence now knew that silk was not necessary for processioning because caterpillars without the ability to lay silk could still line up and march.

Perhaps more exciting? Terrence now had two sheets of paper with dotted lines recording the exact path the caterpillars that could produce silk and those that could not had recently marched. And, so, he was in the position to ask a new question.

He placed both sheets of white paper—the one with a silk trail and the one without—on a table.

He placed a single pine processionary caterpillar on each, very close to the dotted line. It was as if he were asking that caterpillar:

HAVE THEY LEFT A TRAIL THAT YOU CAN FOLLOW?

On the sheet marked with silk, the new caterpillar found the dotted line and followed it exactly.

On the sheet marked by caterpillars with plugged spinnerets, the sheet with no silk at all, the new caterpillar found the dotted line and followed it exactly, too.

Yes, the two caterpillars said together, *there is a trail*.

Terrence had shown that pine processionary caterpillars could leave a trail that was not made of silk.

But now he wanted to know: Was that trail made of pheromones?

ON MOLTING

Caterpillars are tiny when they first hatch out of their eggs. And by the time they're ready to relax into the pupal stage of life, they're very large. In between, as their bodies grow, they continually molt, shedding their too-small outer exoskeletons to reveal, each time, a new and bigger one underneath. These larger and larger caterpillars are called instars. Different instars of the same species can sport completely different color markings and hair patterns, making caterpillars tricky to identify in the wild. Conveniently, the molting process discarded any glue that Terrence may have placed on a caterpillar's spinneret.

Nine
NO TRAIL

Caterpillars produce pheromones in a gland on their abdomens. These cannot be plugged the way spinnerets can, but Terrence knew from his tent caterpillar work that if he could keep the pheromone-producing gland from touching the surface a caterpillar walked on, he could keep the pheromone from reaching the ground, too. That is, he could prevent the laying of a pheromone trail.

So, Terrence took the same thirty caterpillars whose spinnerets he had already plugged with glue, and he pasted tiny strips of paper over the pheromone-producing area of their abdomen. These caterpillars were now unable to dribble silk *or* to lay pheromones.

You may be wondering if these procedures harmed the caterpillars. The honest answer is that we don't know for sure. We do know that the glue placed on spinnerets falls off during the molting process, and the caterpillars go back to dribbling silk. We also know that the strips of paper are shed during the caterpillar's next molt.

And because Terrence took these thirty experimental caterpillars and placed them on a clean sheet of paper in his laboratory, we know this, too: caterpillars that cannot lay silk or pheromones are still able to follow one another in a line.

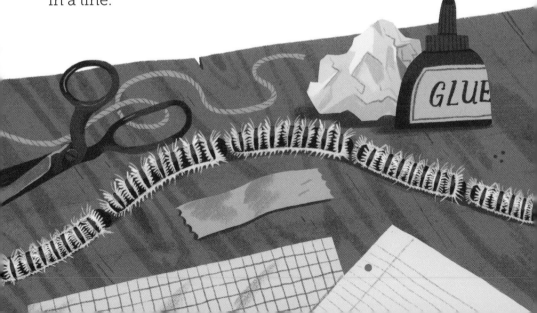

As Terrence watched his thirty silk-less, pheromone-less caterpillars march across a fresh piece of white paper, processioning just as their normal counterparts do, he marked their trail with a dotted pencil line, as usual.

When they'd finished, he removed the caterpillars from the page.

Then he took a new caterpillar and placed it on the paper, very close to the dotted line. He stepped back and waited to see what that new caterpillar would do.

That caterpillar wandered the page aimlessly.

It did not find the dotted line.

It never found any trail at all.

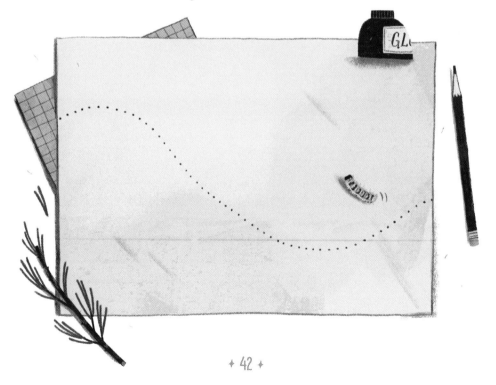

Ten

A SACRIFICE

Terrence's experiments suggested that silk and pheromones were important trail-marking tools for pine processionary caterpillars.

His experiments also made it clear that silk and pheromones were not important to the marching habit itself. (Remember that silk-less, pheromone-less caterpillars, placed together on white paper, lined up and marched with no problem.) What, then, drove the processionary instinct?

Terrence had a theory.

He thought that pine processionary marching might be based on *touch*.

And because he was a thinker and an asker of questions—a scientist—Terrence had already thought of an experiment to test this theory. But he'd have to sacrifice a caterpillar to do it.

If you are squeamish, or if the death of a caterpillar will make you sad or angry, what comes next will be hard to read. Still, if you are intensely curious and can accept the sacrifice of a few caterpillars in order to under-stand the habits of the many, a mystery that humans have been studying for hundreds of years in backyards and laboratories all over the world, then read on. And know that no scientist ever takes such an experiment lightly.

To test the theory that long lines of marching pine processionaries were stimulated by touch, Terrence killed a caterpillar and cut it in half.

Then he scooped the insides out of one of the halves.

Then he put the emptied skin around the end of a thin stick.

And *then* he took a fresh sheet of paper and put a handful of pine processionary caterpillars on its surface. Immediately the caterpillars formed a procession and began to march across the page. This time, Terrence ignored the caterpillar at the end of the line because he wasn't interested in following the procession. This time, he wanted to *lead it*.

Terrence touched the caterpillar-coated end of his stick to the head of the procession line leader.

And the very instant that he did, the leader ceased its usual thrashing about. The leader became a follower, marching placidly behind Terrence's caterpillar-stick decoy. As did all the caterpillars in the long line behind.

"I could lead a procession in any direction by moving it [the decoy] slowly in front of the leader. Moreover, I was able to do the same with a model made from a completely unrelated species of caterpillar."

RAILROAD STORIES

Processionary and other social caterpillars go mostly unnoticed until their huge numbers or their chosen path (or both!) cross with humans. In a remarkable example from 1913, the *New York Times* reported that "billions" of caterpillars had climbed onto the metal bars of the Long Island Rail Road tracks between the Amagansett and Montauk stations and had stayed there, marching east en masse. There were so many caterpillars on the tracks that when a train came through and inadvertently squished them, their bodies greased the tracks beyond passage. The trains were stopped for days as the caterpillars were cleared and new ones, marching steadily from the woods surrounding the track, were exterminated. The episode was written about as a mere curiosity, but Terrence would later wonder if the caterpillars on the rails held clues about the caterpillars on the rim of clay pots in Henri's greenhouse.

Eleven

TRAPPED!

The processionary marching instinct is strong. The caterpillars will follow one another, they will follow a dead pine processionary body threaded onto a stick, and they will even follow a similar decoy made from the body of a completely different type of caterpillar.

Still, Terrence doubted that they would ignore hunger and exhaustion and freezing temperatures for more than a week, all because of this instinct. In short, he doubted the results of Henri's long-ago circle experiment.

"My suspicion," Terrence wrote about that experiment, "was that the caterpillars were not adhering blindly to their instinct to follow each other but were in effect physically trapped on the rim [of Henri's pot]."

Terrence set out to test this idea with the last of the caterpillars he'd brought home from Spain. He set yet another collection of caterpillars on yet another sheet of paper. Then he took a petri dish—a shallow, circular plate of clear plastic that is a common tool in research laboratories—and he turned it upside down over them. Whenever he did this, the caterpillars made their way to the inner edge of the dish and marched beside it. With some trial and error, Terrence determined that seventeen pine processionaries was the perfect number to form an unbroken, head-to-tail, circular procession that fit within the confines of one overturned standard-size petri dish.

Terrence let the caterpillars march under the petri dish for an hour or so—plenty of time to establish silk and pheromone trails in the shape of a circle along the inside edge of a petri dish.

Then he lifted the petri dish.

If Henri's theory were correct—that is, if a procession-ary caterpillar is driven only by an obsessive instinct to follow the caterpillar in front of it—the seventeen would have marched for days, just as they had on the rim of the pot in Henri's greenhouse.

But they didn't.

Terrence's pine processionaries circled for a short time—about two minutes, on average—and then marched off in one long line. Terrence repeated this experiment many times with many processions of caterpillars, and the results were always the same: the caterpillars would circle for minutes, sometimes hours, but never for days.

Serendipity had led a band of processionaries onto a clay pot in Henri's backyard, and Henri had tricked them into staying there by brushing away the extras and allowing the caterpillars to form a circle on the rim. And it appears that they marched for eight days *not* because of blind instinct, as Henri supposed, but because they have a natural aversion to climbing down from slippery perches. They'd been tricked, yes, but they'd also been trapped.

Conclusion

Science is one long line of learning. Jean-Henri Fabre wasn't the first person to wonder about and study pine processionaries; the French entomologist René Antoine Ferchault de Réaumur (1683–1757) was studying them fifty years before Henri Fabre was even born. And Terrence Fitzgerald won't be the last social-caterpillar scientist, either; he has trained students who study them in places around the world today. The relentless march toward fully understanding the life and habits of the pine processionary caterpillar will continue for as long as these unusual caterpillars and we curious people live together in this world. There will be more questions . . . there will be occasional misunderstandings and missteps . . . and there will be more answers. That's what a line of learning looks like.

But the story of science is so much more than caterpillar conversations.

It's the millions of other insects there are to wonder about, the thousands of insect habits we don't yet understand, the countless habits *we haven't even seen*. It's the things we believe to be true and realize, suddenly, might not be. It's all the other intricate and interesting pieces of the galactic puzzle we live in but haven't fully figured out. Were all dinosaurs feathered? Why are prime numbers special? Is time travel possible? What is the universe made of?

Just think of all the questions waiting to be asked!

Think about who might ask them.

Think about how.

Glossary

ABDOMEN: the hindmost segment of an insect's three-part body; the other two segments are the head and the thorax

CHILL COMA: the temperature at which an organism is no longer able to move or function due to the cold

COMMUNAL: shared by all the members of a community

DIAPAUSE: a period of time during which an insect demonstrates little or no activity, usually in response to environmental conditions

EXOSKELETON: the stiff-but-flexible external covering of an insect's body

EXPERIMENT: a series of actions undertaken to test an idea, demonstrate a fact, or otherwise pursue understanding

EXTERMINATED: killed or destroyed

GLAND: bodily tissue or organ that produces chemical substances

INSTAR: in insect development, the growth stage between two periods of molting

INSTINCT: the innate tendency of an organism to respond to specific events or circumstances in a particular way, without thinking or reasoning

MOLT: in insects, the shedding of an old exoskeleton in order to make way for a larger one that supports new growth

PETRI DISH: a shallow, circular, lidded dish, usually made of clear plastic and commonly found in research laboratories; these dishes are often used to grow microorganisms, although Terrence put them to a very different use in the experiments described in this book

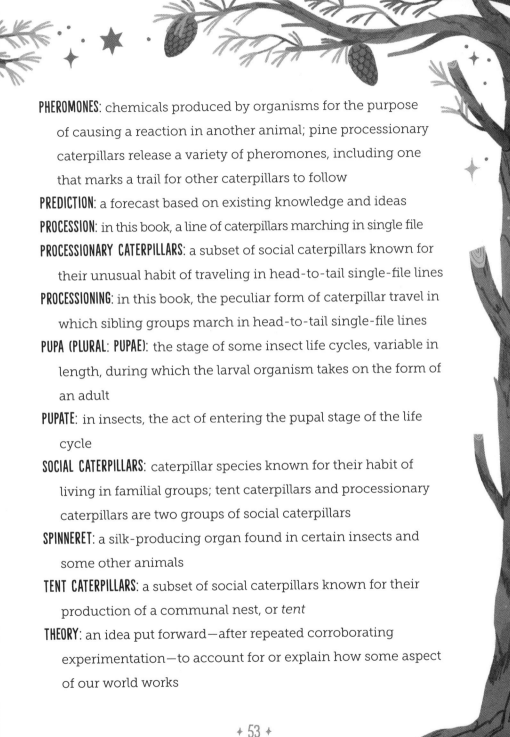

PHEROMONES: chemicals produced by organisms for the purpose of causing a reaction in another animal; pine processionary caterpillars release a variety of pheromones, including one that marks a trail for other caterpillars to follow

PREDICTION: a forecast based on existing knowledge and ideas

PROCESSION: in this book, a line of caterpillars marching in single file

PROCESSIONARY CATERPILLARS: a subset of social caterpillars known for their unusual habit of traveling in head-to-tail single-file lines

PROCESSIONING: in this book, the peculiar form of caterpillar travel in which sibling groups march in head-to-tail single-file lines

PUPA (PLURAL: PUPAE): the stage of some insect life cycles, variable in length, during which the larval organism takes on the form of an adult

PUPATE: in insects, the act of entering the pupal stage of the life cycle

SOCIAL CATERPILLARS: caterpillar species known for their habit of living in familial groups; tent caterpillars and processionary caterpillars are two groups of social caterpillars

SPINNERET: a silk-producing organ found in certain insects and some other animals

TENT CATERPILLARS: a subset of social caterpillars known for their production of a communal nest, or *tent*

THEORY: an idea put forward—after repeated corroborating experimentation—to account for or explain how some aspect of our world works

More about Jean-Henri Fabre and Terrence Fitzgerald

French Museum of Natural History at Jean-Henri Fabre's home: www.harmasjeanhenrifabre.fr/fr

Terrence Fitzgerald's online archive of social caterpillar knowledge: https://web.cortland.edu/fitzgerald/

Terrence Fitzgerald's pine processionary caterpillar web page: https://facultyweb.cortland.edu/fitzgerald/PineProcessionary .html

Further Reading

Alexander, Lori. *All in a Drop: How Antony van Leeuwenhoek Discovered an Invisible World*. Illustrated by Vivien Mildenberger. New York: Houghton Mifflin Harcourt, 2019.

Engle, Margarita. *Summer Birds: The Butterflies of Maria Merian*. Illustrated by Julie Paschkis. New York: Holt, 2010.

Sidman, Joyce. *The Girl Who Drew Butterflies: How Maria Merian's Art Changed Science*. New York: Houghton Mifflin Harcourt, 2018.

Smith, Matthew Clark. *Small Wonders: Jean-Henri Fabre & His World of Insects*. Illustrated by Giuliano Ferri. Seattle: Two Lions, 2015.

Source Notes

p. 5: "By February . . . upon them": Fabre, *The Life of the Caterpillar*, 67.

p. 10: "Where the first goes . . . front of it": ibid., 58.

p. 12: "When the procession . . . white ribbon": ibid., 59.

p. 23: "The procession will go . . . somewhere or other": ibid., 74.

p. 24: "All follow mechanically . . . a watch": ibid., 75.

p. 26: "inimitable observer": Darwin, *The Origin of Species*, 95.

p. 26: "the insect's Homer": Fabre, *The Life of Jean Henri Fabre*, 3–4.

p. 30: "To date . . . any detail": Fitzgerald, "Social Caterpillars," hosted by SUNY at Cortland and maintained by Terrence D. Fitzgerald, https://web.cortland.edu /fitzgerald/.

p. 34: "a poisoned fabric . . . handle it": Fabre, *The Life of the Caterpillar*, 133.

p. 34: "there were few . . . dermatitis": Fitzgerald, "Lethal Fuzz," 31.

p. 45: "I could lead a procession . . . species of caterpillar": ibid., 32–33.

p. 46: "billions": "Railroad Wars."

p. 47: "My suspicion . . . on the rim": Fitzgerald, personal communication with the author, July 26, 2021.

Bibliography

Darwin, Charles. *The Origin of Species*. New York: Mentor/Putnam Penguin, 1958.

Eberle, Irmengarde. *Wide Fields: The Story of Henri Fabre*. New York: Thomas Y. Crowell, 1943.

Fabre, Augustin. *The Life of Jean Henri Fabre: The Entomologist*. Translated by Bernard Miall. London: Hodder and Stoughton, 1910.

Fabre, Jean-Henri. *The Insect World of J. Henri Fabre*. Translated by Alexander Teixeira de Mattos. Introduction and interpretive comments by Edwin Way Teale. Boston: Beacon Press, 1991.

——. *The Life of the Caterpillar*. Translated by Alexander Teixeira de Mattos. New York: Dodd, Mead, 1916.

——. *The Story Book of Science*. Translated by Florence Constable Bicknell. Chapel Hill, NC: Yesterday's Classics, 2006.

Fitzgerald, Terrence D. "Lethal Fuzz." *Natural History*, September 2008, 28–33.

——. "Role of Trail Pheromone in Foraging and Processionary Behavior of Pine Processionary Caterpillars *Thaumetopoea pityocampa*." *Journal of Chemical Ecology* 29, no. 3 (March 2003): 513–532, https://doi.org/10.1023/A: 1022875102682.

Fitzgerald, Terrence D., and Xavier Panades i Blas. "Mid-Winter Foraging of Colonies of the Pine Processionary Caterpillar *Thaumetopoea pityocampa*." *Journal of the Lepidopterists' Society* 57, no. 3, 161–167.

Haskell, Ann. "A Poet of Science Who Saw the World in a Grain of Sand." *Smithsonian*, March 1984, 140.

Howard, L. O. "A Pilgrimage to the Home of Fabre." *Natural History*, July/August 1922, 319–325.

Legros, Georges Victor. *Fabre, Poet of Science*. Translated by Bernard Miall. London: T. Fisher Unwin, 1921.

"Railroad Wars on Caterpillars That Delay Trains." *New York Times*, July 6, 1913.

Wagner, David L. *Caterpillars of Eastern North America*. Princeton: Princeton University Press, 2005.

Wohlleben, Peter. *The Hidden Life of Trees: What They Feel, How They Communicate*. Vancouver: Greystone, 2016.

About the Author

Loree Griffin Burns is a biologist and the author of many nonfiction books for children, including *Honeybee Rescue: A Backyard Drama* and *Life on Surtsey: Iceland's Upstart Island*. Her books have won numerous accolades, including American Library Association Notable designations, a *Boston Globe–Horn Book* Honor, an IRA Children's Book Award, and a Green Earth Book Award, and have twice won the AAAS/Subaru Prize for Excellence in Science Books. She lives in central New England, where she writes, teaches, and studies her insect neighbors.

About the Illustrator

Jamie Green is the illustrator of multiple books for young readers, including *Mushroom Rain* by Laura K. Zimmermann, and was the 2019 Society of Illustrators Zankel Scholar. Their work explores themes of science, history, fun, and all things that crawl. Jamie Green lives just west of Chicago and can often be found foraging in local parks or lifting at the gym.